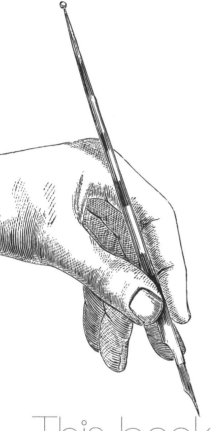

This book belongs to :

_____

LEARN Handwriting WITH JOKES

Welcome to a handwriting journey like no other! In this unique handwriting joke book, we embark on a quest to improve your penmanship and add a dash of humor and creativity along the way. We'll start with essential handwriting tips and advice, setting the foundation for your progress. Then, you'll delve into letter practice to hone your skills. But here's the twist: we'll sprinkle in short jokes to keep you entertained and engaged. And for the grand finale, we'll challenge you with long riddles to write, fostering both your handwriting finesse and your sense of humor. Get ready to master the art of writing with a grin and a giggle!

Seaside Study

TABLE OF CONTENTS

10 tips to improve handwriting

1. Posture Matters

Sit up straight with both feet flat on the ground. Good posture supports proper alignment of your hand and wrist, making it easier to control your movements.

2. Relax Your Grip

Hold your pen or pencil gently, with your fingers forming a tripod grip (thumb and two fingers). Avoid gripping too tightly, which can lead to fatigue and cramped fingers.

3. Consistency is Key

Strive for consistent letter size and spacing. This uniformity makes your handwriting more legible and aesthetically pleasing.

4. Sloped Writing

Angle your paper slightly to the left if you're right-handed and to the right if you're left-handed. This allows your hand to move more freely and reduces smudging.

5. Practice Letter Formation

Pay attention to how each letter is formed. Consistent and correct letter formation is vital for legibility. Utilize lined paper to help with letter height and spacing.

6. Slow Down

Take your time when writing. Rushing can lead to sloppy handwriting. As you practice, you'll naturally become faster without sacrificing quality.

7. Use the Right Tools

Choose a pen or pencil that feels comfortable in your hand. Experiment with different writing instruments until you find the one that best suits you.

8. Warm-Up Exercises

Before writing, do a few warm-up exercises to loosen your hand and wrist. Simple doodles and loops on your paper can help prepare your muscles for writing.

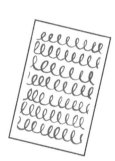

9. Patience and Perseverance

Remember that improving your handwriting takes time. Be patient with yourself, and don't get discouraged by initial challenges.

10. Seek Feedback

Ask friends, family, or teachers to review your handwriting and offer constructive feedback. Sometimes, an outside perspective can help identify areas for improvement.

Chapter 1

In this chapter, we'll dive into the building blocks of good handwriting letter formation. So, grab your favorite pen or pencil, and let's get started on the path to impeccable penmanship! In this chapter, students will learn the steps to master the fundamentals of writing each letter of the alphabet. Through a series of engaging exercises and activities, learners will be introduced to the basic strokes and shapes necessary for forming clear and legible letters. Each letter will be broken down step-by-step, providing ample opportunities for practice and reinforcement. By the end of this chapter, learners will have gained the confidence and skills needed to write each letter independently with precision and clarity.

Let's get started.

Print Alphabet

 A a

a a a a a a a

a a a a a a a

a

A A A A A A A A

A A A A A A A A

A

alligator

A B C D E F G H I J K L M N O P Q R S T U V W X Y Z

B↓ ²→ B↘ b↓ ²→

b b b b b b b

b b b b b b b

b

B B B B B B B

B B B B B B B

B

bear

A B C D E F G H I J K L M N O P Q R S T U V W X Y Z

7

C c

Follow the dots to trace the letters, then write them neatly in the open space provided.

C   c   c   c   c   c   c

c   c   c   c   c   c   c

c

C   C   C   C   C   C   C

C   C   C   C   C   C   C

C

cat

A B C D E F G H I J K L M N O P Q R S T U V W X Y Z

8

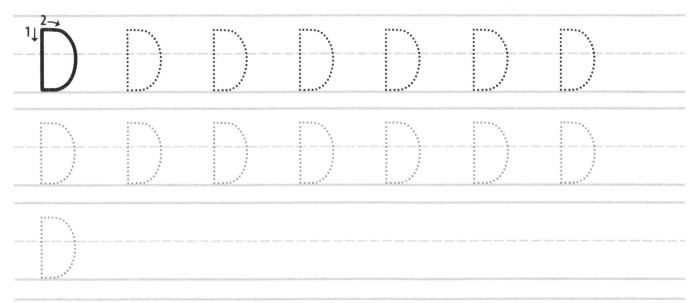

deer

A B C **D** E F G H I J K L M N O P Q R S T U V W X Y Z

E e

Follow the dots to trace the letters, then write them neatly in the open space provided.

e e e e e e e

e e e e e e e

e

E E E E E E E

E E E E E E

E

elephant

A B C D E F G H I J K L M N O P Q R S T U V W X Y Z

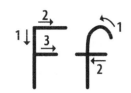

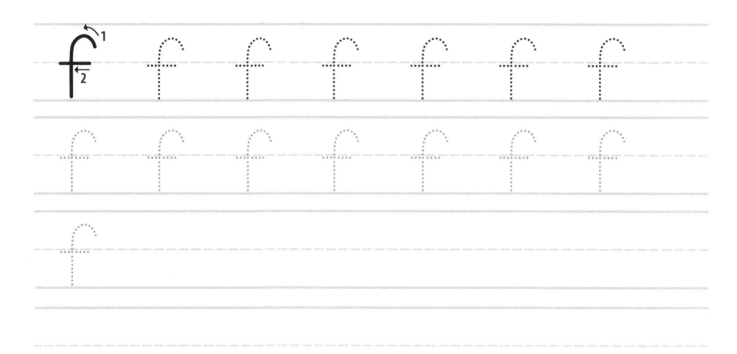

f f f f f f

f f f f f f

f

F F F F F F

F F F F F F

F

A B C D E **F** G H I J K L M N O P Q R S T U V W X Y Z

11

flamingo

G g

g g g g g g g

g g g g g g g

g

G G G G G G

G G G G G G

G

goat

A B C D E F **G** H I J K L M N O P Q R S T U V W X Y Z

12

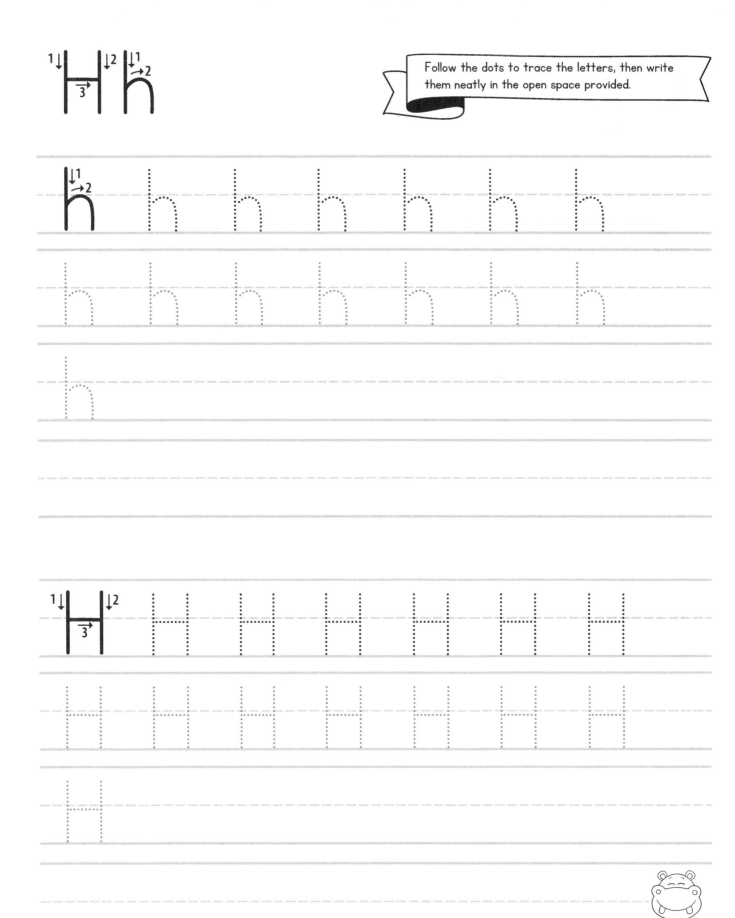

Follow the dots to trace the letters, then write them neatly in the open space provided.

hippopotamus

A B C D E F G H I J K L M N O P Q R S T U V W X Y Z

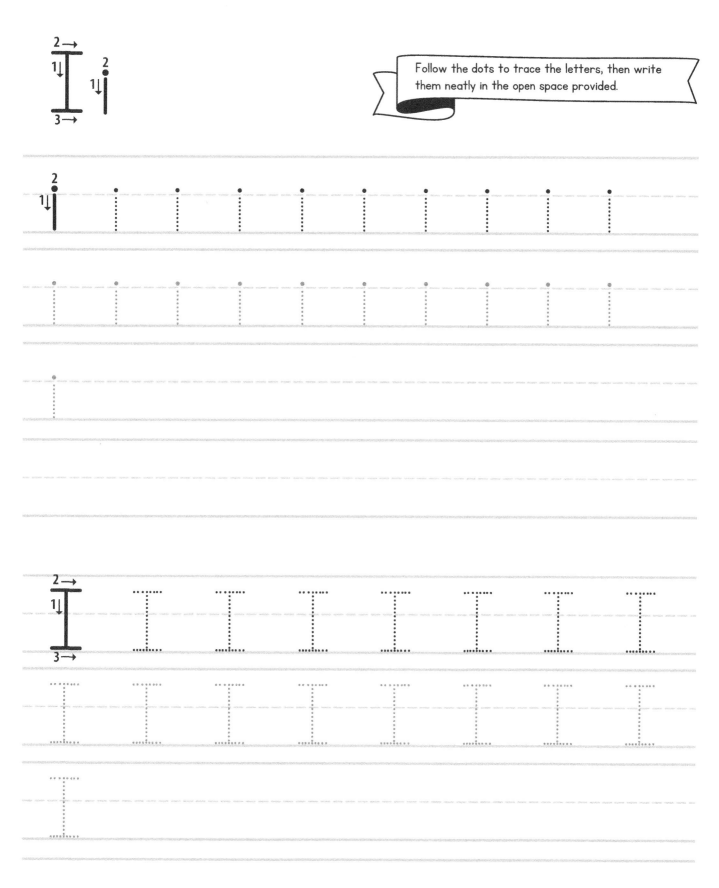

I I I I I I I

A B C D E F G H I J K L M N O P Q R S T U V W X Y Z

iguana

Follow the dots to trace the letters, then write them neatly in the open space provided.

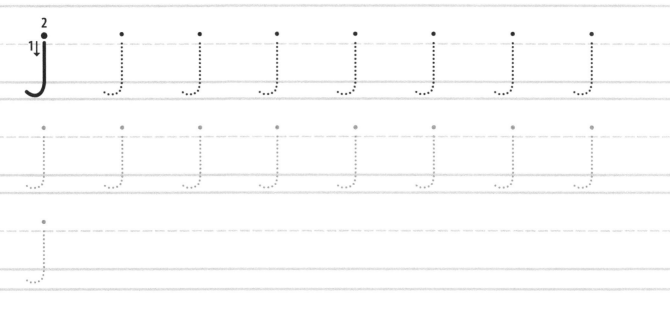

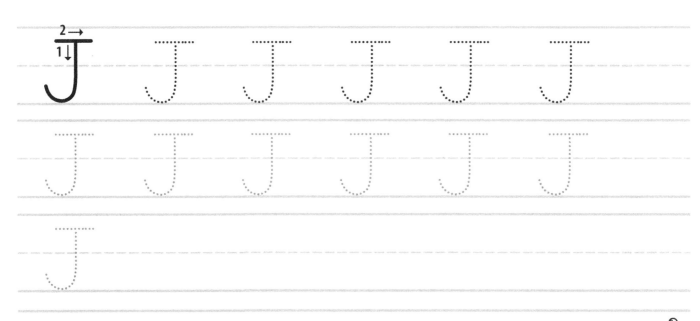

jellyfish

A B C D E F G H I J K L M N O P Q R S T U V W X Y Z

k   k   k   k   k   k   k

k   k   k   k   k   k   k

k

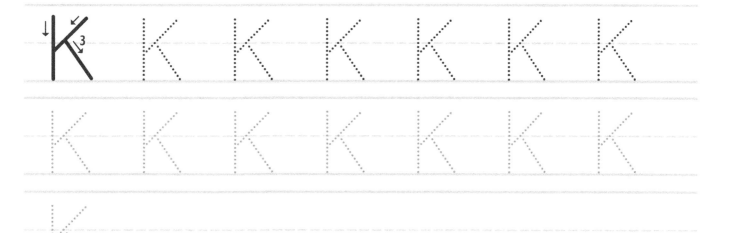

K   K   K   K   K   K   K

K   K   K   K   K   K   K

K

koala

A B C D E F G H I J **K** L M N O P Q R S T U V W X Y Z

1↓   ↓
2→

↓ | | | | | | | | | | |

1↓
2→

A B C D E F G H I J K **L** M N O P Q R S T U V W X Y Z

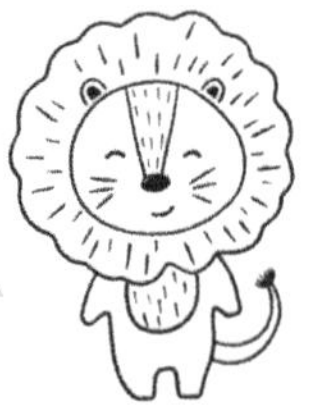

lion

17

 M m

m m m m m m

m m m m m m

m

M M M M M M

M M M M M M

M

monkey

A B C D E F G H I J K L M N O P Q R S T U V W X Y Z

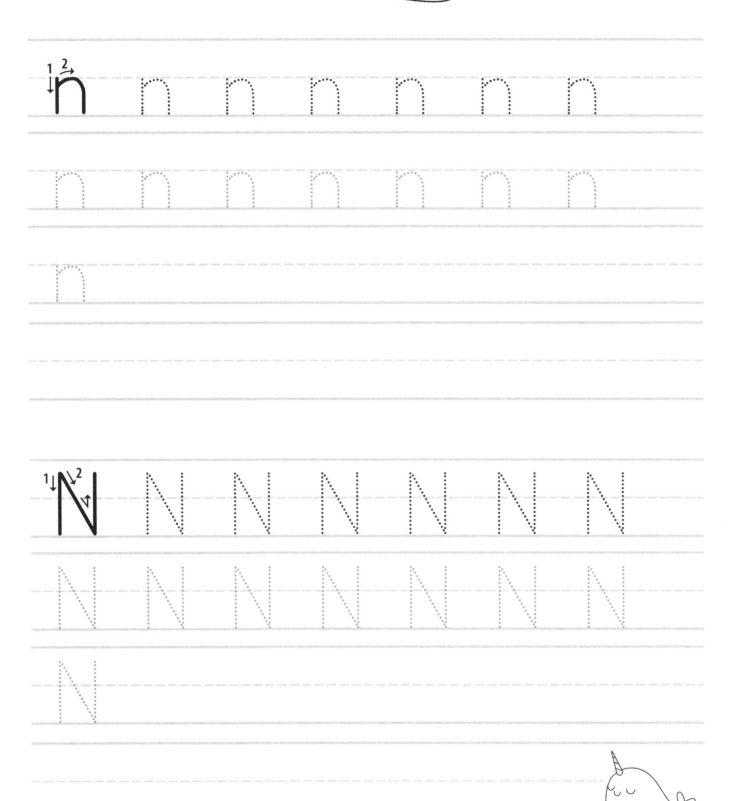

narwhal

A B C D E F G H I J K L M N O P Q R S T U V W X Y Z

O o

Follow the dots to trace the letters, then write them neatly in the open space provided.

A B C D E F G H I J K L M N O P Q R S T U V W X Y Z

octopus

20

p p p p p p p

p p p p p p p

p

P P P P P P P

P P P P P P P

P

pig

A B C D E F G H I J K L M N O P Q R S T U V W X Y Z

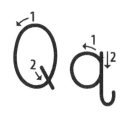

Follow the dots to trace the letters, then write them neatly in the open space provided.

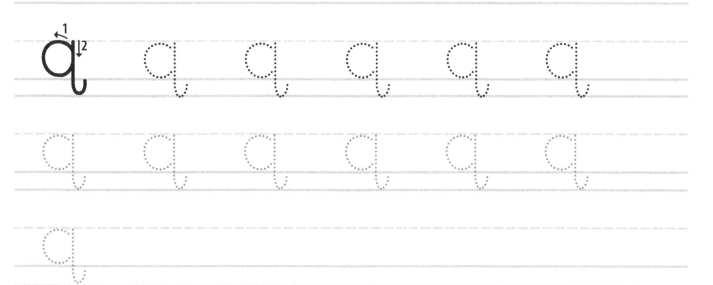

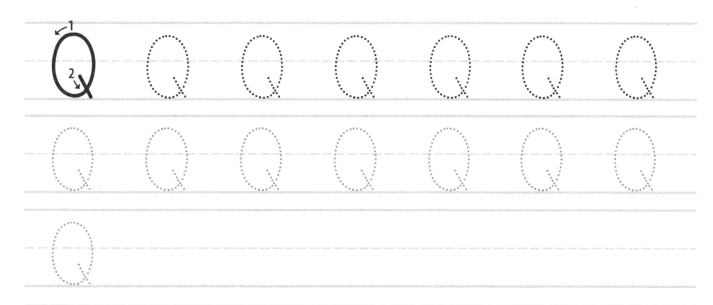

quail

A B C D E F G H I J K L M N O P Q R S T U V W X Y Z

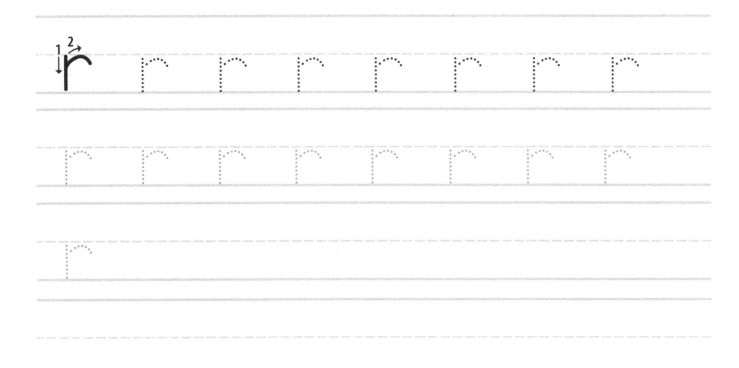

A B C D E F G H I J K L M N O P Q R S T U V W X Y Z

rabbit

Ss

Follow the dots to trace the letters, then write them neatly in the open space provided.

s s s s s s s s

s s s s s s s s

s

S S S S S S S

S S S S S S

S

A B C D E F G H I J K L M N O P Q R **S** T U V W X Y Z

snake

24

turtle

 U u

Follow the dots to trace the letters, then write them neatly in the open space provided.

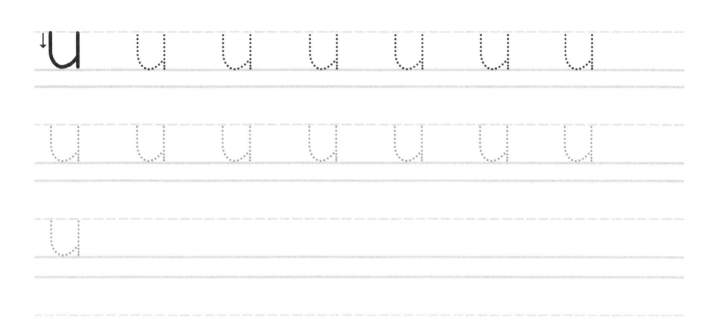

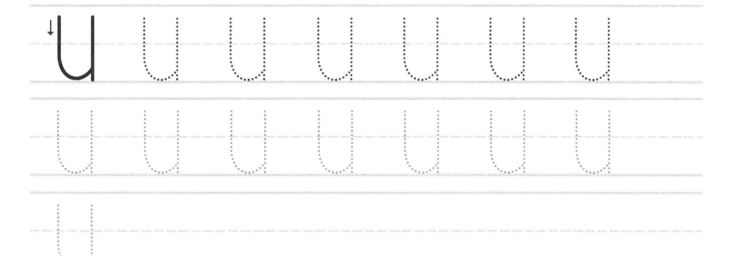

unicorn

A B C D E F G H I J K L M N O P Q R S T U V W X Y Z

V V V V V V V

V V V V V V V

V

V V V V V V

V V V V V V

V

A B C D E F G H I J K L M N O P Q R S T U V W X Y Z

vulture

Follow the dots to trace the letters, then write them neatly in the open space provided.

W   w   w   w   w   w

w   w   w   w   w   w

w

W   W   W   W   W

W   W   W   W   W

W

whale

A B C D E F G H I J K L M N O P Q R S T U V W X Y Z

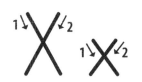

X   X   X   X   X   X   X

X   X   X   X   X   X   X

X

X   X   X   X   X   X   X

X   X   X   X   X   X   X

X

x-ray fish

A B C D E F G H I J K L M N O P Q R S T U V W X Y Z

Follow the dots to trace the letters, then write them neatly in the open space provided.

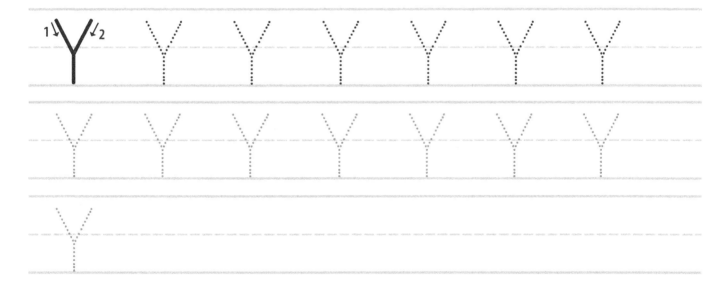

yak

A B C D E F G H I J K L M N O P Q R S T U V W X Y Z

Z z

Follow the dots to trace the letters, then write them neatly in the open space provided.

Z Z Z Z Z Z Z

Z Z Z Z Z Z Z

Z

Z Z Z Z Z Z Z

Z Z Z Z Z Z Z

Z

zebra

A B C D E F G H I J K L M N O P Q R S T U V W X Y Z

31

Chapter 2

Jokes

Welcome to Chapter 2 of our handwriting book, where the pen meets humor! Get ready for a dose of laughter as we explore the fun side of learning to write. In this chapter, we'll provide you with short jokes to trace and write, giving your handwriting skills a delightful twist. Not only will you be mastering the art of penmanship, but you'll also have some side-splitting jokes up your sleeve. So, grab your pen, prepare to giggle, and let's dive into the world of hilarious handwriting practice!

Let's have some fun!

Read the joke

How do you make a hot dog stand?

Take away its chair!

Trace the joke

How do you make a hot dog
stand?

Take away its chair!

Write the joke

A B C D E F G H I J K L M N O P Q R S T U V W X Y Z

Read the joke

Why do flamingos stand on one leg? If they lifted the other leg, they would fall over!

Trace the joke

Why do flamingos stand on
one leg?
If they lifted the other leg,
they would fall over!

Write the joke

A B C D E F G H I J K L M N O P Q R S T U V W X Y Z

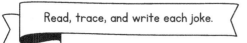

Read the joke

What did the little corn say to the mama corn?

Where is pop corn!

Trace the joke

What did the little corn say to
the mama corn?

Where is pop corn!

Write the joke

A B C D E F G H I J K L M N O P Q R S T U V W X Y Z

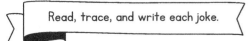

Read the joke

Why can't a leopard hide?

Because he is always spotted!

Trace the joke

Why can't a leopard hide?

Because he is always spotted!

Write the joke

A B C D E F G H I J K L M N O P Q R S T U V W X Y Z

Read the joke

What do you call a bear without any teeth?

A gummy bear!

Trace the joke

What do you call a bear
without any teeth?

A gummy bear!

Write the joke

A B C D E F G H I J K L M N O P Q R S T U V W X Y Z

Read the joke

What did one volcano say to the other?

I lava you.

Trace the joke

What did one volcano say to the other?

I lava you.

Write the joke

A B C D E F G H I J K L M N O P Q R S T U V W X Y Z

Read the joke

Why is six afraid of seven?

Because seven eight nine.

Trace the joke

Why is six afraid of seven?

Because seven eight nine.

Write the joke

A B C D E F G H I J K L M N O P Q R S T U V W X Y Z

Read the joke

Why did the pony get sent to his room?
He wouldn't stop horsing around!

Trace the joke

Why did the pony get sent to his room?
He wouldn't stop horsing around!

Write the joke

A B C D E F G H I J K L M N O P Q R S T U V W X Y Z

Read the joke

What do you call a sad
strawberry?
A blueberry!

Trace the joke

What do you call a sad
strawberry?
A blueberry!

Write the joke

A B C D E F G H I J K L M N O P Q R S T U V W X Y Z

Read the joke

Why did the scarecrow win an award?
He was outstanding in his field!

Trace the joke

Why did the scarecrow win an award?
He was outstanding in his field!

Write the joke

A B C D E F G H I J K L M N O P Q R S T U V W X Y Z

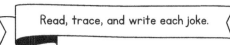

Read the joke

What did one ocean say to the other ocean?

Nothing, it just waved!

Trace the joke

What did one ocean say to

the other ocean?

Nothing, it just waved!

Write the joke

A B C D E F G H I J K L M N O P Q R S T U V W X Y Z

Read the joke

How can you keep someone in
suspense?
I'll tell you tomorrow!

Trace the joke

How can you keep someone in
suspense?
I'll tell you tomorrow!

Write the joke

A B C D E F G H I J K L M N O P Q R S T U V W X Y Z

Read the joke

Why are cats good at video games? Because they have nine lives.

Trace the joke

Why are cats good at video games? Because they have nine lives.

Write the joke

A B C D E F G H I J K L M N O P Q R S T U V W X Y Z

Read the joke

What did the left eye say to the right eye?
Between us, something smells.

Trace the joke

What did the left eye say to
the right eye?
Between us, something
smells.

Write the joke

A B C D E F G H I J K L M N O P Q R S T U V W X Y Z

Read the joke

Why do birds fly south for the winter?

It's too far to walk!

Trace the joke

Why do birds fly south for the winter?

It's too far to walk!

Write the joke

A B C D E F G H I J K L M N O P Q R S T U V W X Y Z

Read the joke

Why do we never tell secrets on a farm?

Because the corn has ears!

Trace the joke

Why do we never tell secrets
on a farm?

Because the corn has ears!

Write the joke

A B C D E F G H I J K L M N O P Q R S T U V W X Y Z

Read the joke

Why do bees have sticky hair?

Because they always use honeycombs!

Trace the joke

Why do bees have sticky hair?

Because they always use

honeycombs!

Write the joke

A B C D E F G H I J K L M N O P Q R S T U V W X Y Z

Read the joke

Why was the science teacher angry?

He was a mad scientist!

Trace the joke

Why was the science teacher angry?

He was a mad scientist!

Write the joke

A B C D E F G H I J K L M N O P Q R S T U V W X Y Z

Read the joke

What is as big as an elephant but weighs zero pounds? The elephants shadow!

Trace the joke

What is as big as an elephant but weighs zero pounds? The elephants shadow!

Write the joke

ABCDEFGHIJKLMNOPQRSTUVWXYZ

Read the joke

Why did the bird go to the library?
It was looking for bookworms!

Trace the joke

Why did the bird go to the
library?
It was looking for
bookworms!

Write the joke

A B C D E F G H I J K L M N O P Q R S T U V W X Y Z

Read the joke

What kind of bugs read the
dictionary?
Spelling bees!

Trace the joke

What kind of bugs read the
dictionary?
Spelling bees!

Write the joke

A B C D E F G H I J K L M N O P Q R S T U V W X Y Z

55

Read the joke

What kind of key opens a banana?
A mon-key!

Trace the joke

What kind of key opens a
banana?
A mon - key!

Write the joke

A B C D E F G H I J K L M N O P Q R S T U V W X Y Z

Read the joke

What has two legs but can't walk?

A pair of pants!

Trace the joke

What has two legs but can't walk?

A pair of pants!

Write the joke

A B C D E F G H I J K L M N O P Q R S T U V W X Y Z

Read the joke

What do you call a dinosaur with bad vision?
A Do-you-think-he-sarus!

Trace the joke

What do you call a dinosaur with bad vision?

A Do - you - think - he - sarus !

Write the joke

A B C D E F G H I J K L M N O P Q R S T U V W X Y Z

Read the joke

Why did the cow go to space?

To see the moooon!

Trace the joke

Why did the cow go to space?

To see the moooon!

Write the joke

A B C D E F G H I J K L M N O P Q R S T U V W X Y Z

Read the joke

What is a bats motto?

Hang in there!

Trace the joke

What is a bats motto?

Hang in there!

Write the joke

ABCDEFGHIJKLMNOPQRSTUVWXYZ

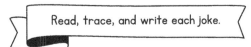

Read the joke

How do you get a squirrel to like you?

Act like a nut.

Trace the joke

How do you get a squirrel to like you?

Act like a nut.

Write the joke

A B C D E F G H I J K L M N O P Q R S T U V W X Y Z

Read the joke

What animal is always at a baseball game? A bat.

Trace the joke

What animal is always at a baseball game? A bat.

Write the joke

A B C D E F G H I J K L M N O P Q R S T U V W X Y Z

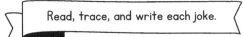

Read the joke

Where do polar bears vote?

The North Poll!

Trace the joke

Where do polar bears vote?

The North Poll!

Write the joke

A B C D E F G H I J K L M N O P Q R S T U V W X Y Z

Read the joke

What kind of lion never roars?

A dandelion.

Trace the joke

What kind of lion never roars?

A dandelion.

Write the joke

A B C D E F G H I J K L M N O P Q R S T U V W X Y Z

Read the joke

Why could the bicycle not stand up by itself?

It was two-tired!

Trace the joke

Why could the bicycle not stand up by itself?

It was two-tired!

Write the joke

A B C D E F G H I J K L M N O P Q R S T U V W X Y Z

Read the joke

Where do polar bears keep their money? In a snow bank!

Trace the joke

Where do polar bears keep their money? In a snow bank!

Write the joke

A B C D E F G H I J K L M N O P Q R S T U V W X Y Z

Read the joke

What do you call a dinosaur
that is sleeping?
A dino - snore!

Trace the joke

What do you call a dinosaur
that is sleeping?
A dino - snore!

Write the joke

A B C D E F G H I J K L M N O P Q R S T U V W X Y Z

Read the joke

Why did the elephant bring a suitcase to the zoo?

It wanted to pack its trunk!

Trace the joke

Why did the elephant bring a

suitcase to the zoo?

It wanted to pack its trunk!

Write the joke

ABCDEFGHIJKLMNOPQRSTUVWXYZ

Read the joke

What do you call a sleeping bull?

A bull-dozer!

Trace the joke

What do you call a sleeping bull?

A bull-dozer!

Write the joke

A B C D E F G H I J K L M N O P Q R S T U V W X Y Z

Read the joke

Why did the teddy bear say no to dessert? Because she was stuffed.

Trace the joke

Why did the teddy bear say no to dessert? Because she was stuffed.

Write the joke

A B C D E F G H I J K L M N O P Q R S T U V W X Y Z

Chapter 3

Riddles

Welcome to Chapter 3 of our handwriting adventure! In this section, we're taking your writing skills to the next level by adding a dash of mystery and mirth. Here, you'll find funny riddles to trace and then craft on your own. These witty challenges aren't just brain teasers but also fantastic tools for honing your ability to write longer passages with grace and style. So, grab your trusty pen and prepare for a journey of laughs, riddles, and eloquent penmanship. Let's dive into the art of turning chuckles into beautifully written words!

Trace the riddle

I have a shiny black-and-white coat, and I love to waddle around in the cold. My favorite food is fish, and I sometimes slide on my belly to get where I want to go.

What am I?

Write the answer

A B C D E F G H I J K L M N O P Q R S T U V W X Y Z

Write the riddle

Write the answer

Answer: A penguin

A B C D E F G H I J K L M N O P Q R S T U V W X Y Z

Trace the riddle

I am tall when I am young, and I can stretch and bend without breaking. People often find me in the most colorful places, and I love to sway in the breeze.

What am I?

Write the answer

A B C D E F G H I J K L M N O P Q R S T U V W X Y Z

Write the riddle

Write the answer

Answer: A flower

A B C D E F G H I J K L M N O P Q R S T U V W X Y Z

Trace the riddle

I have a long, bushy tail
and a mask - like pattern
on my face. I am known
for being crafty and
sneaky, and I love to
climb trees.

What am I?

Write the answer

A B C D E F G H I J K L M N O P Q R S T U V W X Y Z

Write the riddle

Write the answer

A B C D E F G H I J K L M N O P Q R S T U V W X Y Z

Trace the riddle

I am made of metal and have hands, but I can not move on my own. People often use me to tell the time, and I chime with a pleasant sound.

What am I?

Write the answer

A B C D E F G H I J K L M N O P Q R S T U V W X Y Z

Write the riddle

Write the answer

Answer: A clock

A B C D E F G H I J K L M N O P Q R S T U V W X Y Z

Trace the riddle

I am a type of vehicle that travels on tracks, and I carry both passengers and freight. People often use me for long journeys, and I am known for my distinct "choo - choo" sound.

What am I?

Write the answer

A B C D E F G H I J K L M N O P Q R S T U V W X Y Z

Write the riddle

Write the answer

Answer: A train

A B C D E F G H I J K L M N O P Q R S T U V W X Y Z

Trace the riddle

I am a place filled with books of all kinds, and people come to borrow them for a while. You can find stories and knowledge here, and I am often a quiet and peaceful space.

What am I?

Write the answer

A B C D E F G H I J K L M N O P Q R S T U V W X Y Z

Write the riddle

Write the answer

Answer: A library

A B C D E F G H I J K L M N O P Q R S T U V W X Y Z

Trace the riddle

I am a creature with wings and often associated with magical stories. People believe I grant wishes and leave a trail of sparkling dust wherever I go.

What am I?

Write the answer

A B C D E F G H I J K L M N O P Q R S T U V W X Y Z

Write the riddle

Write the answer

Answer: A fairy

A B C D E F G H I J K L M N O P Q R S T U V W X Y Z

Trace the riddle

I am a delicious treat that comes in many flavors and colors. People enjoy licking me on hot days, and I can sometimes be served in a cone or a cup.

What am I?

Write the answer

A B C D E F G H I J K L M N O P Q R S T U V W X Y Z

Write the riddle

Write the answer

Answer: Ice cream

A B C D E F G H I J K L M N O P Q R S T U V W X Y Z

Trace the riddle

I am a game played on a large green field that involves hitting a small white ball with a club. People try to get the ball into a series of holes using the least number of strokes.

What am I?

Write the answer

A B C D E F G H I J K L M N O P Q R S T U V W X Y Z

Write the riddle

Write the answer

Answer: Golf

A B C D E F G H I J K L M N O P Q R S T U V W X Y Z

Trace the riddle

I am a season that comes
after summer, and I bring
falling leaves and cooler
weather. People often
dress up in costumes and
go trick - or - treating
during this time.

What am I?

Write the answer

A B C D E F G H I J K L M N O P Q R S T U V W X Y Z

Write the riddle

Write the answer

Answer: Autumn

A B C D E F G H I J K L M N O P Q R S T U V W X Y Z

Chapter 4

Free Writing

Welcome to the creative heart of our handwriting book! Here, we give you the space to let your imagination run wild. It's your chance to practice handwriting and craft your own jokes and riddles. Think of it as a playground for your pen, where the rules are flexible, and the only limit is your own creativity. So, grab your pen and let your thoughts flow onto the page. This chapter is all about exploring your unique voice and giving life to your very own humor and wit. Let's embark on this exciting journey to create, laugh, and pen your way to handwriting mastery!

Ää Bb Cc Dd Ee Ff Gg Hh Ii Jj Kk Ll Mm Nn Oo Pp Qq Rr Ss Tt Uu Vv Ww Xx Yy Zz

95

Ää Bb Cc Dd Ee Ff Gg Hh Ii Jj Kk Ll Mm Nn Oo Pp Qq Rr Ss Tt Uu Vv Ww Xx Yy Zz

Aa Bb Cc Dd Ee Ff Gg Hh Ii Jj Kk Ll Mm Nn Oo Pp Qq Rr Ss Tt Uu Vv Ww Xx Yy Zz

97

Aa Bb Cc Dd Ee Ff Gg Hh Ii Jj Kk Ll Mm Nn Oo Pp Qq Rr Ss Tt Uu Vv Ww Xx Yy Zz

Ää Bb Cc Dd Ee Ff Gg Hh Ii Jj Kk Ll Mm Nn Oo Pp Qq Rr Ss Tt Uu Vv Ww Xx Yy Zz

Aa Bb Cc Dd Ee Ff Gg Hh Ii Jj Kk Ll Mm Nn Oo Pp Qq Rr Ss Tt Uu Vv Ww Xx Yy Zz

Please

Leave a review

Thanks so much for using **Learn Handwriting With Jokes**. We are a family company creating books for kids just like ours. It would mean a lot to us if you left an honest review of our book. As a hard working self-publishing company, reviews help to get the word out. We want to hear what you have to say and so do others! Leaving an Amazon review is a quick and easy way to help pass on handwriting skills to a new generation.

Thank You!

Seaside Study

Made in the USA
Las Vegas, NV
16 March 2024